DATE DUE

D1371851

What happens when you

RUN?

WHAT HAPPENS WHEN . . .?

What Happens When You Breathe?
What Happens When You Catch a Cold?
What Happens When You Eat?
What Happens When You Grow?
What Happens When You Hurt Yourself?
What Happens When You Listen?
What Happens When You Look?
What Happens When You Run?
What Happens When You Sleep?
What Happens When You Talk?
What Happens When You Think?
What Happens When You Touch and Feel?

Library of Congress Cataloging-in-Publication Data

Richardson, Joy.
    What happens when you run?
    (What happens when — ?)
    Bibliography: p.
    Includes index.
    Summary: Describes how the bones, muscles, lungs, and other parts
of the body work together when a person runs.
    1. Running — Physiological aspects — Juvenile literature.
[1. Running — Physiological aspects] I. Maclean, Colin,
1930-   ill. II. Maclean, Moira, ill. III. Title. IV. Series:
Richardson, Joy. What happens when — ?
QP310.R85R53 1986   612'.76   86-3707
ISBN 1-55532-135-6
ISBN 1-55532-110-0 (lib. bdg.)

This North American edition first published in 1986 by
Gareth Stevens, Inc.
7317 West Green Tree Road   Milwaukee, Wisconsin 53223, USA

U.S. edition, this format, copyright © 1986
Supplementary text and illustrations copyright © 1986
by Gareth Stevens, Inc.
Illustrations copyright © 1984 by Colin and Moira Maclean

First published in the United Kingdom by Hamish Hamilton Children's
Books with an original text copyright by Joy Richardson.
Typeset by Ries Graphics, ltd.
Series editor: MaryLee Knowlton
Cover design: Gary Moseley
Additional illustration/design: Laurie Shock

What happens when you
RUN?

Joy Richardson

pictures by
Colin and Moira Maclean

introduction by
Gail Zander, Ph.D.

Gareth Stevens Publishing
Milwaukee

. . .a note to parents and teachers

Curiosity about the body begins shortly after birth when babies explore with their mouths. Gradually children add to their knowledge through sight, sound, and touch. They ask questions. However, as they grow, confusion or shyness may keep them from asking questions, and they may acquire little knowledge about what lies beneath their skin. More than that, they may develop bad feelings about themselves based on ignorance or misinformation.

The *What Happens When . . . ?* series helps children learn about themselves in a way that promotes healthy attitudes about their bodies and how they work. They learn that their bodies are systems of parts that work together to help them grow, stay well, and function. Each book in the series explains and illustrates how one of the systems works.

With the understanding of how their bodies work, children learn the importance of good health habits. They learn to respect the wonders of the body. With knowledge and acceptance of their bodies' parts, locations, and functions, they can develop a healthy sense of self.

This attractive series of books is an invaluable source of information for children who want to learn clear, correct, and interesting facts about how their bodies work.

GAIL ZANDER, Ph.D.
CHILD PSYCHOLOGIST
MILWAUKEE PUBLIC SCHOOLS

Ready . . .
Set . . .
Go!

When you run,
all the parts of your body
work together to make you move.

Your bones help you run.
You have long, strong bones in
your arms and legs.

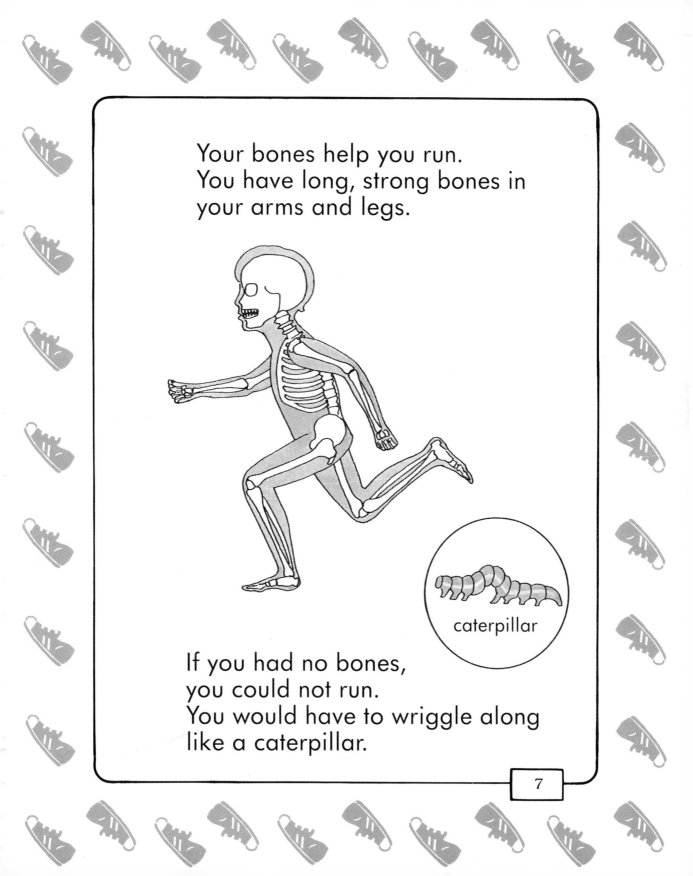

caterpillar

If you had no bones,
you could not run.
You would have to wriggle along
like a caterpillar.

You have joints between your bones
to let you bend.
Some joints are shaped like a hinge.
The bone can only move up and down.
Some joints are shaped like a ball in a cup.
The bone can move around and around.

a hinge joint

a ball joint

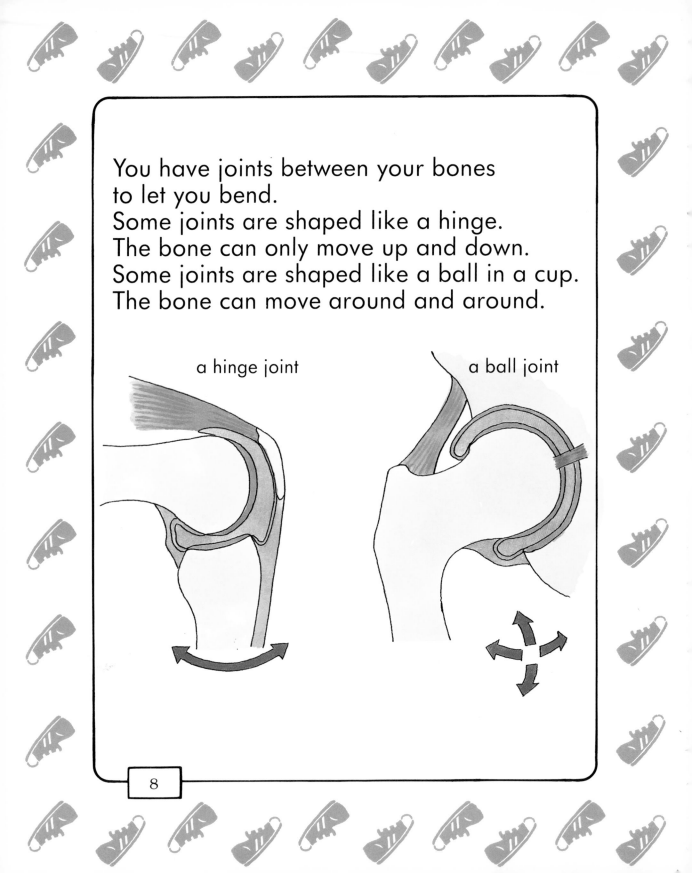

Feel the joints in your
shoulders,
elbows,
hips,
knees.

Can you find four hinge joints
and four ball joints?

Make a ball of clay
on the end of a stick.
Fit the ball into the top of
an eggcup or small teacup
and move the stick
around and around.

Your shoulder and hip joints
work like this.

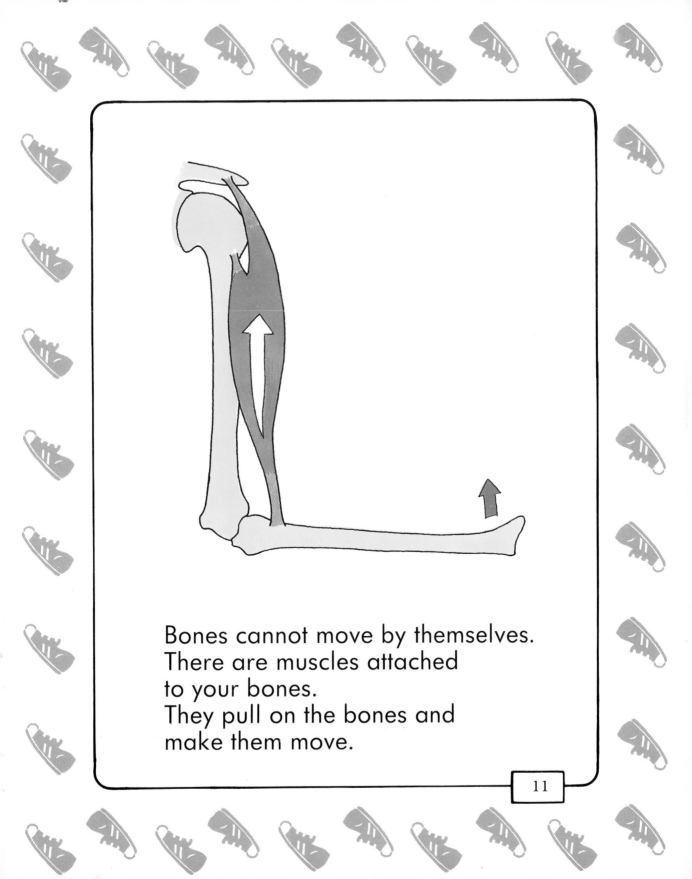

Bones cannot move by themselves.
There are muscles attached
to your bones.
They pull on the bones and
make them move.

11

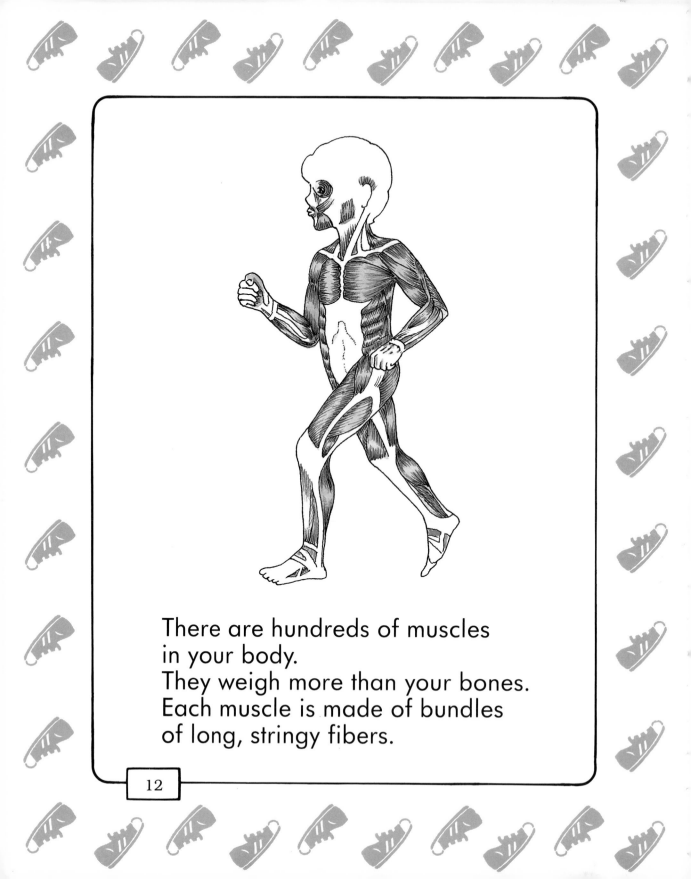

There are hundreds of muscles
in your body.
They weigh more than your bones.
Each muscle is made of bundles
of long, stringy fibers.

Look at a piece of meat.
There may be some skin and
fat on the outside.
The reddish part is made of muscle.
Cut off a small piece and pull it apart.
Look at it under a magnifying glass.
Can you see the stringy fibers?

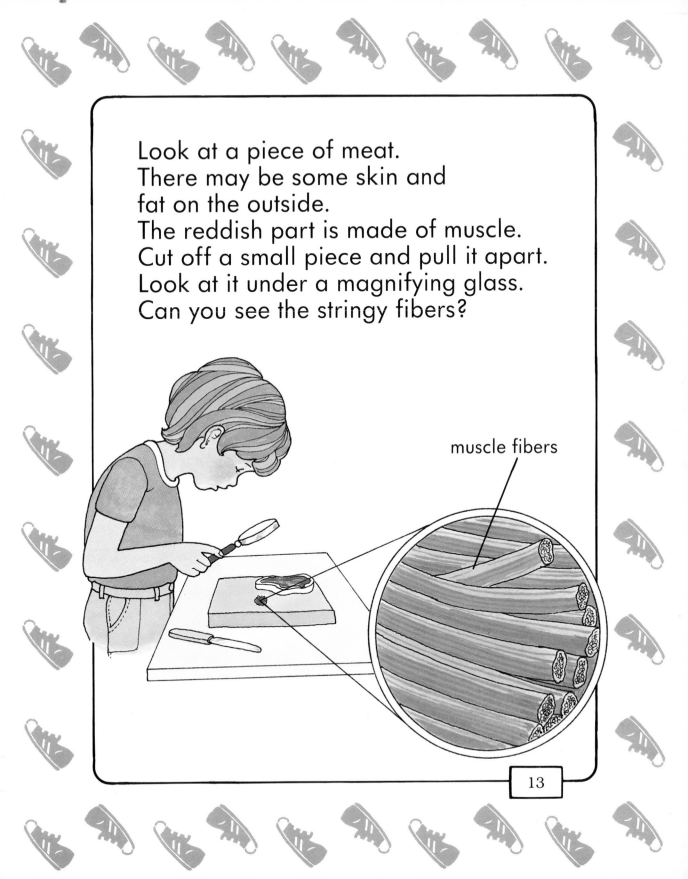

muscle fibers

When you want to move,
your brain sends a message
to your muscles.
The message travels along tiny
threads called nerves.
When it gets to the muscle fibers,
it makes them contract (get shorter).

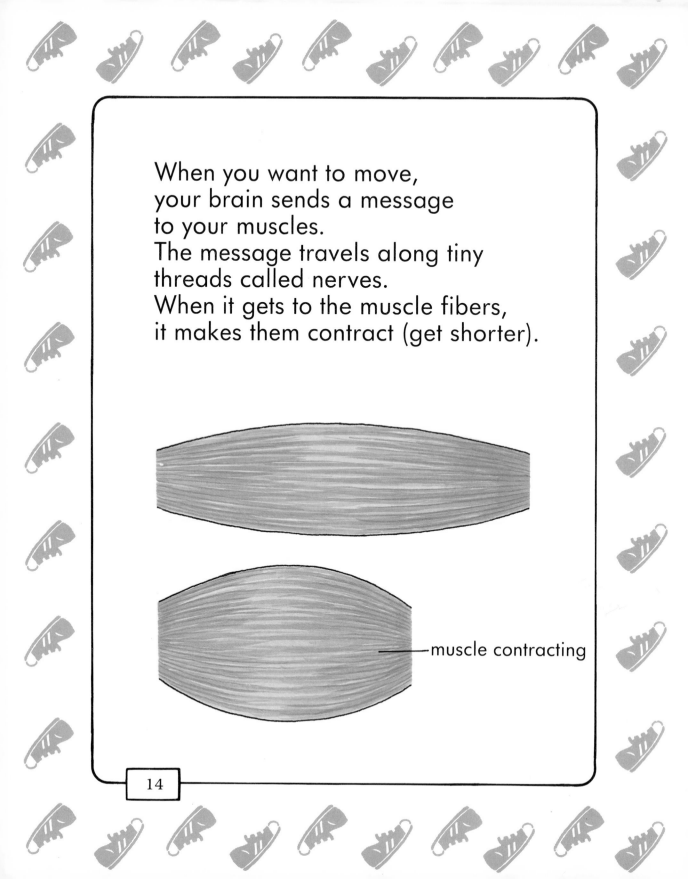

muscle contracting

The muscle fibers get shorter
and fatter.
The muscle bulges in the middle
and tugs on the bone at the far end.

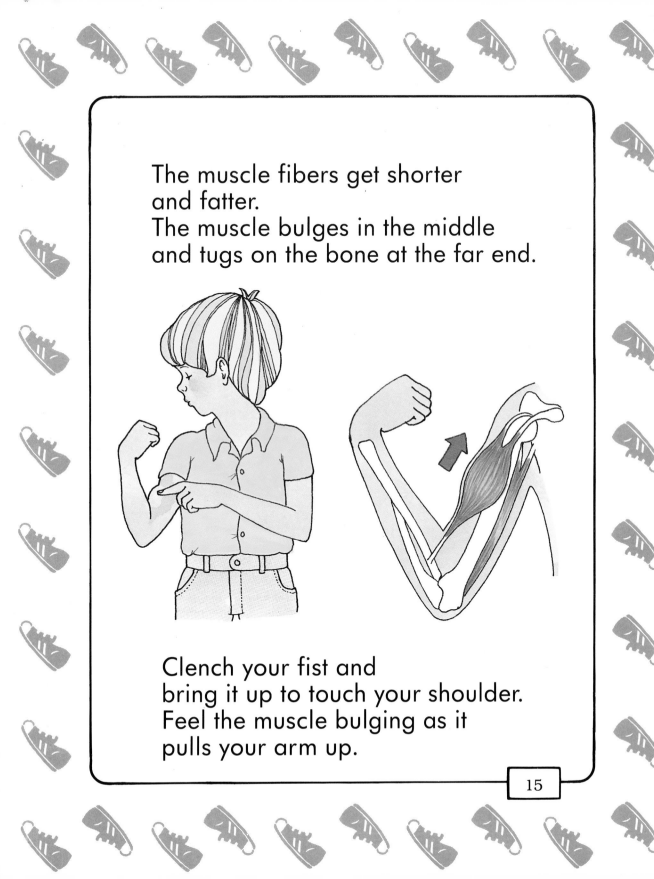

Clench your fist and
bring it up to touch your shoulder.
Feel the muscle bulging as it
pulls your arm up.

Muscles always work in pairs.
When the front muscle on
your upper arm contracts,
it pulls on the lower bone and
bends your arm.

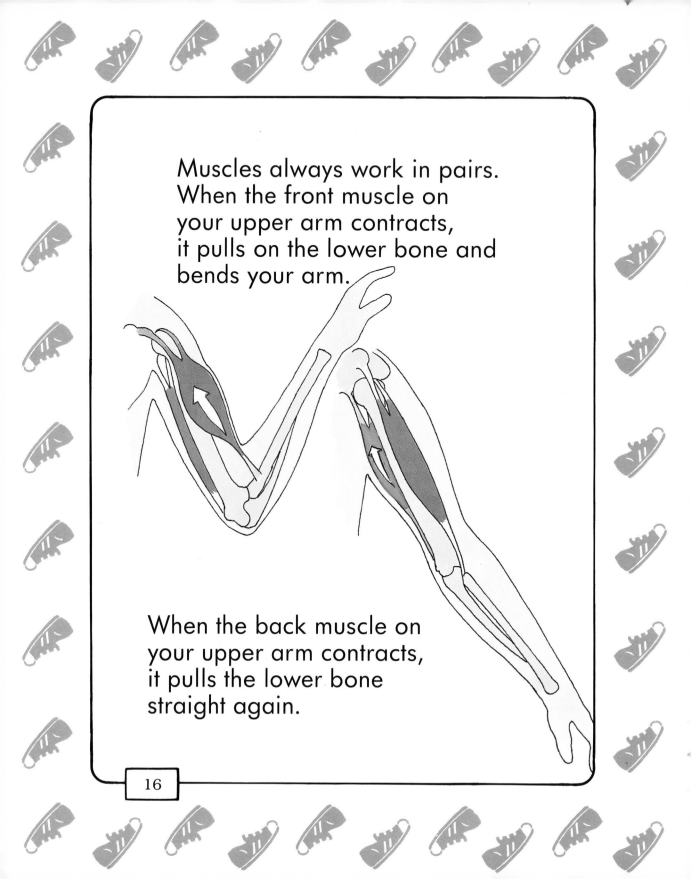

When the back muscle on
your upper arm contracts,
it pulls the lower bone
straight again.

Cut a strip of cardboard to make
an arm. Bend it at the elbow.
Make four small slits like this.
Knot the ends of two pieces of elastic.
Push the elastic through the top slits
to make a muscle on the front and
a muscle on the back.

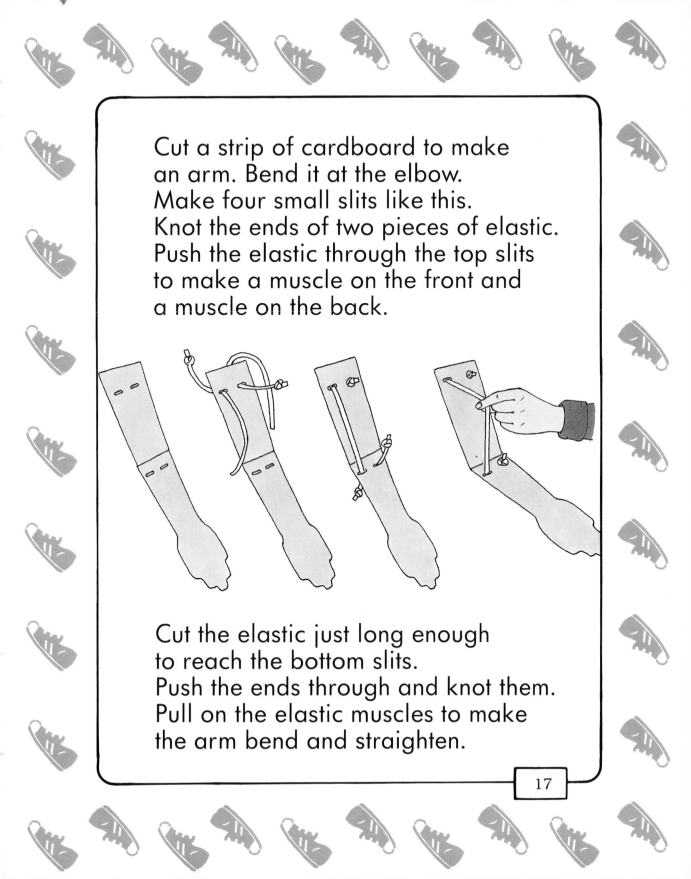

Cut the elastic just long enough
to reach the bottom slits.
Push the ends through and knot them.
Pull on the elastic muscles to make
the arm bend and straighten.

When you start to run,
the big muscle on the
back of your leg contracts.
It pulls on your heel and
lifts it up.
This pushes you forward.

When you run, you bend each leg
and then straighten it again.

Muscles on your hip bone
pull on your thigh bone.
Your leg swings forward and up.

Muscles on the back of your thigh bone
pull on your lower leg bone.
They make you bend your knee.

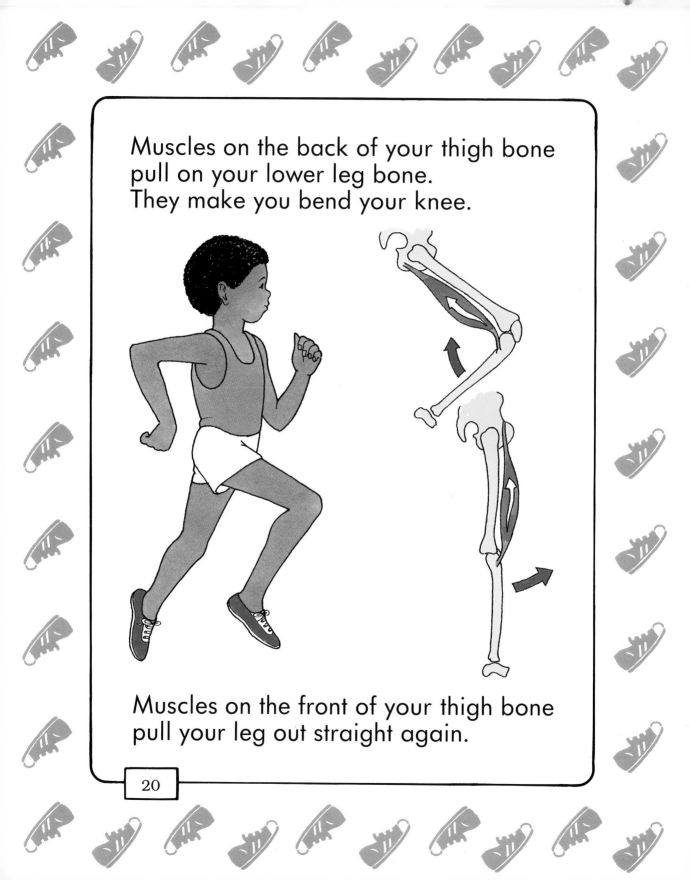

Muscles on the front of your thigh bone
pull your leg out straight again.

Feel your legs to find the muscles
which work when you
bend your knee,
straighten your leg,
stand on your toes.

21

When you run, you move your arms, too.
They swing and push you forward.
They help you to keep your balance.

left arm

right leg

left arm

left leg

Which arm moves with which leg?
Try running like the girl on the left.
Now try running like the boy on the right.
Which way works best?

You need energy for running.
Cars move by turning fuel
into energy.
You move by turning food into energy.

When you make energy, you make heat, too.
So running makes you warm.

Food is stored in your muscles,
ready for use.
Your muscles use oxygen from the air
to turn the food into energy.
Your lungs take in oxygen
from the air you breathe.

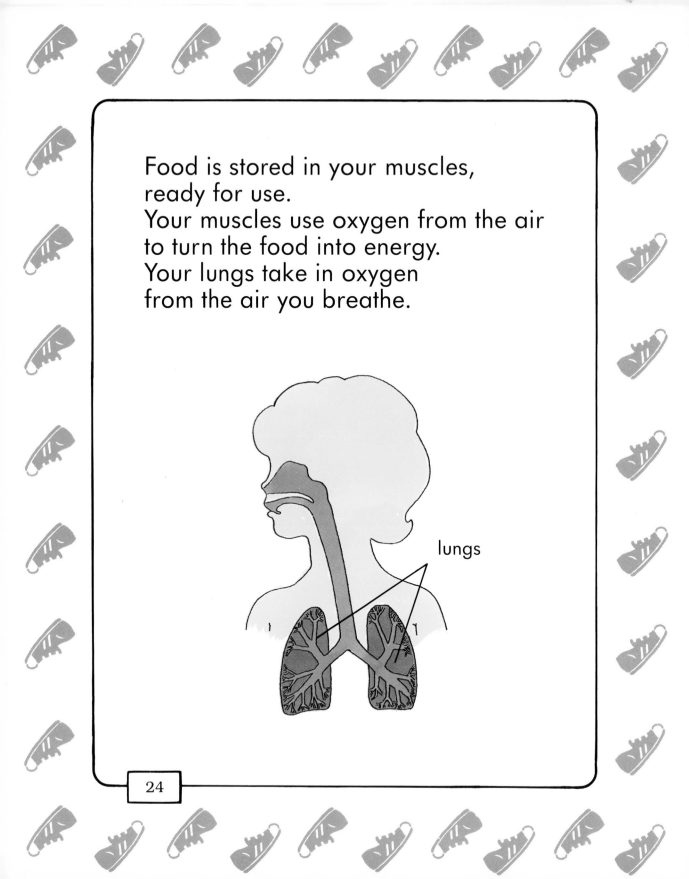

lungs

Put two candles into holders.
Have an adult light the candles
and put a tall jar over one of them.
Which candle goes out first?

The candle in the jar went out when
it had used up all the oxygen
from the air in the jar.
The other candle went on burning
because it could get more oxygen.

A candle needs oxygen to burn wax and
make light.
Your muscles need oxygen
to burn food and make energy.

When your muscles run out of oxygen,
you feel puffed out.
You breathe faster to get more air.

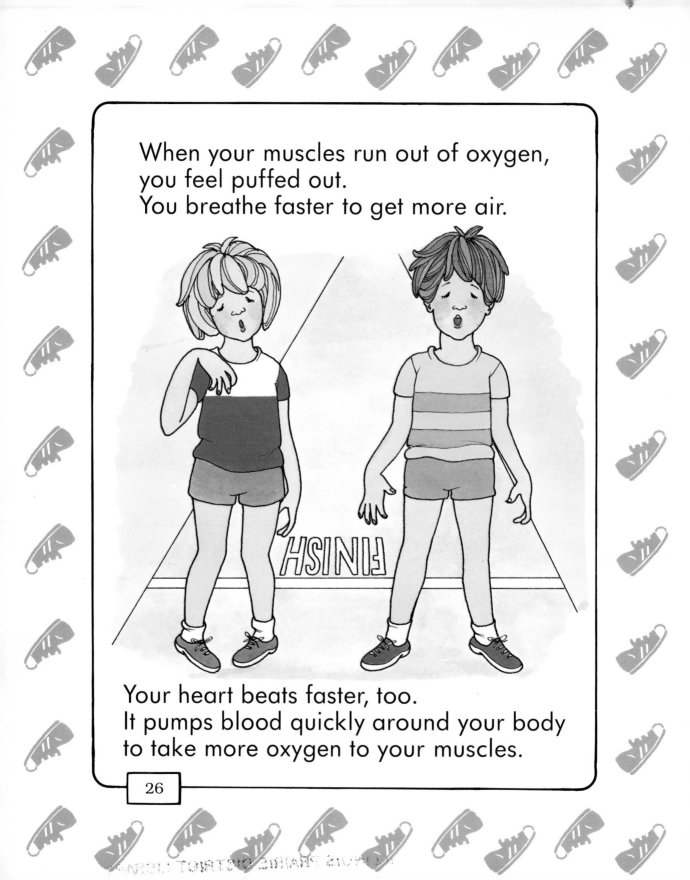

Your heart beats faster, too.
It pumps blood quickly around your body
to take more oxygen to your muscles.

Press with your fingertips on the
thumb side of your wrist.
Each time your heart beats,
you can feel a little thump.
This is called your pulse.

Count how many times
your heart beats in one minute.
Run in place until you feel
puffed out.
Now count your heart beats again
for one minute.

Your heart beats faster when
your muscles need more oxygen.

27

If you run a lot,
your muscles get stronger and
make more energy.
Running helps you keep fit!

28

How Does That Happen?

Did you find all these things to do in *What Happens When You RUN?* If not, turn back to the pages listed here and have some fun seeing how your body works.

1. Find your ball and hinge joints. (page 9)
2. Make a joint from clay. (page 10)
3. Find the muscle in a piece of meat. (page 13)
4. Make your muscle bulge. (page 15)
5. Make an arm with cardboard and elastic. (page 17)
6. Find your leg muscles. (page 21)
7. Try different ways of running. (page 22)
8. See how oxygen works in your muscles. (page 25)
9. Time your heartbeat. (page 27)

More Books About Running

Listed below are more books about what happens when you run. If you are interested in them, check your library or bookstore.

Calico Cat's Exercise Book. Charles (Childrens Press)

From Head to Toes: How Your Body Works. Packard (Simon & Schuster)

Marathon Running. Nentl (Crestwood House)

Run, Run Fast! Sullivan (Crowell)

Running Is for Me. Neff (Lerner)

The Skeleton Inside You. Balestrino (Crowell)

Your Heart and How It Works. Zim (Morrow)

Where to Find More About Running

Here are some people you can write away to for more information about what happens when you run. Be sure to tell them exactly what you want to know about. Include your full name and address so they can write back to you.

American Heart Association
7320 Greenville Avenue
Dallas, Texas 75231

Johnson and Johnson Products, Inc.
501 George Street
New Brunswick, New Jersey 08903

President's Council on Physical Fitness and
    Sports
450 5th Street NW
Washington, D.C. 20001

Special Olympics, Inc.
1350 New York Avenue NW
Suite 500
Washington, D.C. 20005

Index